SHORT STORIES OF A
LIFETIME

Ron DeMarino

WESTBOW
PRESS®
A DIVISION OF THOMAS NELSON
& ZONDERVAN

WestBow Press books may be ordered through booksellers or by contacting:

WestBow Press
A Division of Thomas Nelson & Zondervan
1663 Liberty Drive
Bloomington, IN 47403
www.westbowpress.com
844-714-3454

ISBN: 978-1-6642-5168-7 (sc)
ISBN: 978-1-6642-5167-0 (e)

Library of Congress Control Number: 2021924414

Print information available on the last page.

WestBow Press rev. date: 2/23/2022

BACK TO THE BRONX

I was attending New York University (Downtown Campus), belonging to Air Force R.O.T.C. (Reserve Officers Training Corp) the program teaches college graduates to train to become future officers in the military.

Halfway through my second semester I was attending a training class when a Captain in the Air Force was giving a lecture, at the same time he was really giving me a hard time. This was going on ever since I started the class. It was getting to me, but today I lost my composure having a confrontation with the Captain.

The Captain pressed charges with the court giving me an option, serve time or enlist in the service ... I took the latter.

The following week I am reporting for induction ... going to be stationed at Ft. Dix, New Jersey for my eight weeks of Basic Training, after completion of the eight weeks I received leave. Going back home to the Bronx.

The leave ended my new orders were for me to report back to Ft. Dix starting another eight weeks of Advanced Infantry Training. Nearing the conclusion of my eight weeks, Rumor was spreading that the whole squadron was going to be shipped to Korea. There is an old adage in the service "do not volunteer for anything"

So I volunteered for Leadership school in order not to get shipped off to Korea. In the interim my squadron gets orders to be assigned around the New York State area (Ft.Wadsworth, Ft. Hamilton and Ft. Drum) WOW!!!.

1

I report … assigned to a new basic training company, again at Ft. Dix as a temporary cadre sergeant. The NCO was a staff sergeant in charge of the whole platoon with me being his assistant. The 16 weeks of basic training are complete, orders get issued, it turns out the entire squadron is being shipped to Korea. Had to volunteer!

We were sent to Ft. Lewis, Washington for debarkation to Korea aboard a USS General ship. Landing in Inchon, Korea in June of '54 (the war had ended in July of '53).

We were loaded unto 2 1/2 ton trucks, shipped to general quarters. We had to report to C/A (Classification & Assignments) the whole squadron was assigned to the 3rd Army Infantry Division. It was my turn to approach the sergeant who was handing out the new orders … Seeing that I had gone to Leadership School, he asked me what I would I like to do … I had no idea! So he said I am going to assign you to a company called Civil Affairs which was attached to the 3rd Division MP's. They only have 11 men in the company, two are medical personnel a Dr. who is a Captain and a corpsman. It is run by a 1st Lieutenant … Sounded great!

The only problem was that it was in the Chorwon Valley above the 38th parallel technically in North Korea.

Arrived at Civil Affairs (It was located right next to the 3rd Division MP stockade). Reported to the commanding officer, was issued the 3rd division patch, collar insignias with cross pistols (signifying Military Police) a carbine and a side arm.

We had three squad tents which slept four, we had to sleep on cots with air mattresses. The good part was that we got to eat at The MP cafeteria. We had real milk, fresh eggs and fruit … The 3rd division MP's made a deal with quartermaster not to write them up in order to be granted fresh rations.

We too had stockades it was set in the back of our compound comprising of two squad tents (enclosed in wire) In front of the fence was a four foot wide walk way going around the squad tents was another wired fence in front of the walkway. We also had a fence around our entire perimeter.

The reason for the two stockade tents, was to round up the prostitutes by raiding small villages. We traveled on our patrols with another squad member, a Korean entrepreneur and a Korean Policeman. After arresting the women we would take them back to the first squad tent in which they were tested by the medical team for venereal disease (at least 95% had some form)

The corpsman would then give them one shot a day for a week of penicillin, after being tested negative they would be switched to the second squad tent.

After we had about a dozen women we would truck them down to Seoul handing them over to the Korean Police. There were times we would apprehend the same women multiple times. We also went out on patrol trying to round up slicky slicky boys who were armed gangs that were ravishing there war torn country, trying to steal whatever they can.

When we were not on patrol our other function was to stand guard duty at two separate locations, one was the overall perimeter of our compound the other location was in between the wire fences (the walkway) of the two squad tents. This one night Bob was stationed at the walkway by the squad tents his carbine at his side, while the rest of the company was sleeping (with our carbines at our bed) there was multiple gun shots.

We all jumped out of our beds grabbing our carbines, rushing outside into the night not knowing what we were going to face … As it turned out one of the slicky slicky boys was escaping, as he was going over the second fence Bob opened fire with his carbine not realizing that he had his weapon on automatic fire, unloading the complete banana clip in seconds missing the escaped prisoner. The commanding officer then put out a search party but to avail.

Needless to say our commanding officer was really upset … … The following days we continued to do our job like nothing had transpired.

Until about a month later when I was on guard duty taking care of the exterior perimeter of our compound. A group of slicky, slicky boys were trying to break into the compound wanting to release one of their leaders who we had in our second squad tent being ready for transferring over to the Korean Police in Seoul.

On the far side of the compound away from the MP stockade was a gully about 60 yards from our rear fence which sloped down about three feet and gradually rose up …

That is where I saw movement which I called halt both in English and Korean (Learning a little Korean from our interpreter). They did not comply so I fired off two rounds at the spot where I thought I had last seen them. With this mayhem breaks out as everyone again is outside weapons ready,

We send out a patrol to the area in which I had seen the slicky, slicky boys but no luck, coming up empty. The commanding officer is beside himself so at 2:00 am he has us lined up giving us a chewing out, his last statement was that everyone was going to re-qualify using the carbine. Well it could have been worse. Like canceling our future leave that was going to take place in two weeks, we were going to Japan for R&R (Rest and Recuperation) (but really it was I&I).

Three days later the MP's pulled into our compound delivering a wounded slicky slicky boy with his arm bandaged, stating they had picked him up three nights ago about two miles from our compound. He was treated and handed over to the MP's who in turn was turning him over to us to deal with. After further questioning from our entrepreneur, finding out he was one member of the gang that had tried to free our prisoner. With that knowledge I asked the commanding officer since I did shoot him can we call off the re-qualifying He snapped back certainly not!

So off to qualifying we all passed with Bob barely making it.

It was time to go on R&R as Bob and I went to Osaka, Japan having a great time, I meeting a Eurasian gal having a wild seven days, before you know it is back to Korea and Civil Affairs.

The months roll by, it is the middle of December orders came in stating that the colors of the 3rd division are being transferring back to the states. That means we will be getting new orders ... Now what?

Back to C&A, this time they transfer me to the 185th Military Police Division to be stationed in Taegu, Korea. My new job is to protect the Neutral Nations Investigation Team when they travel throughout Korea, inspecting K bases. Making sure that no one was stock piling any extra war supplies.

The Neutral Nation Teams were made up of four countries ... two neutral (Sweden & Switzerland) and two communist (Poland & Czechoslovakia).

Great duty, as I moved into a building that had been headquarters for high ranking personal during the 2nd world war. Cannot believe I finally have a real bed to sleep in with a bathroom and shower.

But best of all I had a houseboy who took care of my laundry, which included ironing my dress uniform along with my fatigues, shinning my brass and shoes so they looked like glass, making my bed each morning. Costing me a carton a cigarettes each week.

In March of '55 we were driving two of the inspectors, when Rob driving the jeep not recognizing the black ice on the road, the next thing you know we were sliding down an embankment smashing up the jeep. Coming out of the accident with minor bruises. One of the injuries I received was an abrasion under my left eye. The wound started to heal with the scab coming off only to be raw again, this kept on recurring as it would never heal; now causing the area to start weeping. It became a rash continuing to spread now on my hands … It was only affecting the areas exposed to the air. Off to the hospital in Taegu staying there about three weeks not getting any better. Then I was transferred to the hospital in Pusan as I did no better … The wounds would clear up and then break out all over again … So now I was transferred to Tokyo General Hospital. It seemed that whatever they did helped my problem, so I was cleared for active duty being assigned to an MP unit in Tokyo. The day I was supposed to report to my new unit I broke out again.

Time to ship me home with my first stop Tripler Medical Hospital in Hawaii then on to St. Albans Naval Hospital in Queens, New York.

Finally after a month at St. Albans I finally cleared up to be assigned back to active duty … Receiving orders to report to Ft. Devens in Massachusetts, but first I had 10 days leave, back to the Bronx staying with my parents until it was time to report for my new orders. Upon arriving in Ft. Devens, reporting to C&A the Sargent looking up my records states you have more leave coming so I start another 10 days back to the Bronx. My parents were quite surprised in seeing me back again.

Leave is over, back to Ft. Devens don't you know it is a repeat as I have 10 more days left of leave, again back to the Bronx … again surprising my parents which they thought it was getting to be quite comical.

Back to Ft. Devens, this time I only have five days left before I get discharged. The Army did not want to issue me any class A uniforms having just a few days left to serve … so I received green fatigues. What to do with me? I get assigned KP duty (Kitchen Patrol); reporting to a new 2nd Lieutenant who assigns me Pots & Pans. No way … … Telling the Lt. I'm not going to do pots & pans … he says this is a direct order soldier, my answer to him is take your direct order and shove it. Things are getting worse (have to neutralize this situation) so I proceeded to tell him I was just released from the hospital being sent back from Korea with a skin condition … The Lt. mellowed out asking me how about peeling potatoes … Deal I replied, as my army life ended with me peeling potatoes during my last five days … Then it was

BACK to the BRONX.

A GOLDEN OPPORTUNITY

I left NYC in 1960 arriving in Hollywood, CA with my buddy Barry. We rented a two bedroom apartment in Hollywood on Hollywood Blvd. near La Brea.

We met a young man named John who we befriended. His father owned a great Italian restaurant off of La Brea near Melrose. We were going to the restaurant at least once a week … It was expensive.

As it turned out both of us had obtained good jobs … I with an Architect and Engineering company; Barry with one of the studios … so we can afford to eat out quite often.

One night we were out at our favorite Italian restaurant, John the owner's son approaches our table asking if he can join us. The three of us start talking about the jobs we have. I mention that I love to do cartooning as a hobby, such characters like Mickey Mouse, Bugs Bunny etc. John mentions that he would love to see them.

The following week we met I had my portfolio of about fifteen drawings that John looked at … stating that they are wonderful. He told me that Hanna & Barbera studios were just a few buildings down from the restaurant and that both Mr. Hanna and Mr. Barbera come to the restaurant quite often for lunch. He then asked me If he can borrow the portfolio so he can show them my drawings, I complied.

John called me saying that Mr. Barbera is going to call me to set up an appointment for an interview; which he did. With this news I contacted my mother back in NYC to tell her that I have a future interview with Hanna & Barbera. My mother called my grandmother who in turn calls my cousin who just finished making a movie for Columbia pictures, from the novel he wrote Black Board Jungle. My cousin signed a contract with Columbia Studios having an option to make movies on his next three future publications.

As it turns out Hanna & Barbera are with Screen Gems which is a subsidiary of Columbia Studios.

The day of my interview is here with Mr. Barbera at his La Brea Ave studios. The secretary calls me into Mr. Barbera office and the first thing Mr. B said

"I guess you are trying to pull some strings" (I have no idea what he is implying). He proceeds to tell me he received a letter from my cousin's agent stating that whatever he could do for me would be gratefully appreciated. Mr. B then takes out the letter signed by my cousin and his agent and shows it to me … I have no idea that this letter has been sent with me stipulating the same.

The meeting continues with Mr. B looking over my drawings. Now I have added more drawings to the portfolio (Quick Draw McGraw, Yogi Bear and Huckleberry Hound). Mr. B looks over the sketches saying they are quite good. He then states that they are moving the studio to Burbank in a few weeks and he has to go to New York as they will be finalizing a new sponsor … The same time they will be creating a new character (Which was Top Cat).

Mr. B continues to say I would like to meet back with you in about a month seeing what position we can offer you, as our new studio will be ready … Sounded great!

Cannot wait for the time to come … a new career in their new studio

Unfortunately it never came to fruition. I was dating a beautiful up and coming Hollywood actress thinking maybe we would be able to share a future together.

When one day she says she is leaving me, I am devastated, it can't be true! It seemed surreal ... What to do? Have to forget? Get away? Leave California?

That's exactly what I did that week. Going back to New York City ... Leaving behind my past and possibly a wonderful future. Not looking back ... losing

ON A SUMMER DAY

It was on a Saturday in the Bronx, I had to meet the bus by a parking lot on Fordham Road and the Grand Concourse the bus was going to take us to Sing-Sing prison. We were to play the prison baseball team. Our team was made up of 16 players all from our semi-pro baseball league. All our players had been released from there minor league facilities. What made it really nice was the one hour trip to Ossining where the prison is located was that two of my cousins were on the bus ... Cousin Billy was signed by the Boston Braves pitching for the AA affiliate the Austin Braves, Cousin Frankie was drafted by the Cleveland Indians playing with there A ball affiliate ... You have to remember that at this time there was six different classes of baseball up to the majors starting with classes AAA AA A B C and D so if you are in AA ball you are just a few steps away from the bigs.

So here we are on the bus heading to Sing-Sing. Out of the 16 players 4 are pitchers, one of them is also a 1st baseman who happened to be my cousin Billy.

The manager did not want to pitch Billy as he was really wild or right on. There were some minor league games when he would walk 13 or 14 then he would turn it around and strike out as many ... he did not want to take the chance in case he was wild pitching against the prison team ... So he opted for my team mate Eddie who pitched for the Chicago Cubs AA affiliate the San Antonio Missions, Eddies dad was also the owner of the Allerton Ave Pool hall.

We arrived at Sing-Sing it was a beautiful day to play baseball, departed the bus, we were met by a prison guard who led us inside the first gate.

Then greeted by the Assist Warden and the Capt. of the Guards. They proceeded to check our bags, we went through a second gate which they told us we were now inside the prison and to follow them. Going through the Guards cafeteria in order to get to the locker room. The Asset Warden gave us a speech on the do's and don'ts. He stated under no circumstances are you to talk to the players (who also are the inmates), he also stated that the playing field is protected from the stands with a wired fence from home plate to both foul lines which the outfield walls are twenty to twenty five foot high. Do not argue with the umpires and finally he said that the inmates are going to cheer for you, we found that quite amazing. Finally we got dressed in every one's home uniforms leaving the locker room to the dugout, on to the field not knowing what to expect as we were all plesantly surprised on how good the field was.

It was a little strange seeing the big wall in the outfield with the guard towers looming and the wire fence holding back the in mates who were cheering for us.

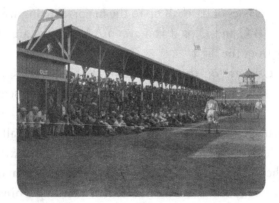

What I did not mention was the S.S for the prison team was from a local neighborhood around Gun Hill Road and Boston Post

Road. He was a very good baseball player, probably would have played minor league ball but if it was not for a home invasion. He and two of his friends; tied up the homeowner gaging him with his own hanky which led to his suffocation … they were all caught and was sentenced to Sing-Sing.

The game started; it really was not much of a game; it was in the 6th inning and we were up by 11 runs 12-1 there run was unearned due to an errant throw by my cousin at S.S. It was 2nd and 3rd with two outs in the 6th, I was coming up to bat (I was already 2-4) the first pitch I fouled straight back, the second pitch was inside for a ball, the third pitch I lost sight of, never picking up the spin as it was heading for my left shoulder, I backed away and naturally the pitch curved over the plate for strike 2. So now I'm guessing the next pitch is going to be a curve ball sure enough it was, but this time I kept my left shoulder in and I drilled a two hop line drive off the wall in left center for a stand up double. So here I'm on 2nd base taking a lead and over my right shoulder I am talking to the SS about the old neighborhood we say a few words the next thing I get picked off of 2nd base … Since it's the third out I get to my position at 3rd with Frankie bringing out my glove and laughing as he did.

Well the final out was a routine ground ball to me with an easy toss to my cousin Billy at 1st. Now we are back in the locker room getting dressed to leave … I'm always the last one dressed and last to leave. So that day was no exception. I was lacing my sneakers when I felt people hovering over me, I looked up it was the Ass't Warden and the Capt. of the Guards. The warden says where do you think you are going, I said to catch the bus he replied no you are not we saw you talking to our S.S. You were told under no circumstances were you to talk to the inmates … So you are not going anywhere because we need a 3rd basement and you are it. At that point I felt like I needed help, can they really do this? Am I really in trouble? What can I do? They stood their ground looming over me which seemed like an hour but in reality it was probably a minute or two.

Then they started to look and each other and started laughing stating get finished dressing and get out of here before we really change our minds.

The 2nd gate closed as I was getting on the bus. Thinking back WHAT A SUMMER DAY!

Ron Marino

Former Kansas City Royals Scout

Semi-Pro Baseball Uniform

A CHRISTMAS DAY

It was a cold winter night in New York City being the later part of January. We were having a real bad cold spell. But my friends and I were still going to the big Latin dance being held at the Hotel New Yorker in Manhattan on 34th Street.

Looking forward to hearing the music from the Latin bands like Toto Puente, Joe Cuba, Tito Rodrigues, Machito and a host of other bands. This night Puente and Rodrigues were performing. When one band finishes a set the other band comes on, as they were on a revolving stage.

Puente did the first set then Tito Rodrigues followed, starting out with a few of his famous boleros that he was noted for … Fronting the band was this pretty looking lady who was doing backdrop singing as well as playing the maracas and the Guira (Weddle). WOW was she stunning!

Marta and Tito Rodrigues

During one of the numbers I was dancing close to the stage trying to get her attention but to no avail. The dance ended with me trying a few more times … did not succeed.

The following week we went to another dance at The Taft Hotel located on 50th St. again in downtown Manhattan. The bands were Tito Rodrigues and Johnny Pocheco. Rodrigues opened the dance again I was near the stage looking up at this pretty lady … trying to get her attention saying remember me from last week not a glance. This occurred with no recognition after two more tries as the dance ended.

The following year on a summer night my friends and I took off to the Palladium located on 53rd street in NYC. The entertainer was Celia Cruz, can't wait to see her in person. After her first set on came a band, it was Tito Rodrigues with the pretty lady fronting the band, trying to get her attention failing again.

In the interim I found out her name was Marta.

This never is going to happen, me trying to meet this pretty lady. I have to stop fantasizing about meeting her and that's what I did.

Life went on dating other gals but never getting quite serious enough to contemplate marriage.

In the summer of 1965 a group of friends decided to move to Southern California living in Hollywood. When one day Barry came over to my apartment and says that Tito Rodrigues is playing at the Hollywood Palladium. So off we go to see Tito; this was their final tour stop after coming off a two week stay at the Rivera in Las Vegas. It was great, no surprise Marta was fronting the band. I got close to the stage looking up towards her, saying Hi do you remember me from New York again there was no response. I tried a second time again no acknowledgement. Oh well I tried!

Things did not work out well living in California so it was back to NYC.

I moved to the Bronx then to Flushing Queens which is a borough of New York City. At that time my good friend Marvin was managing a disco in mid-town Manhattan wanting to make one night Latin night. He asked me if I knew any gals that were pretty and bi-lingual who would like to be a hostess. I replied that there was a pretty lady in my building who would fit his needs.

Marvin said great let me know.

At this time I am decorating my apartment with all Chinese décor. I had the door open and Mary the upstairs neighbor came by wanting to see the progress I was doing in the apartment. The opportunity asking about the disco came up and she replied no, but maybe my sister would be interested. Great now I have to deal with her sister, I asked Mary what her sister looked like, she proceeded to tell me that at one time she was with a Latin band ... I then asked, who was the Latin band? Mary replying Tito Rodrigues. I thought no way!

I said Mary wait a minute going to my record collection and bringing out an album with a picture on the cover with Mary responding that is my sister.

I could not believe this. After so many years trying to meet this lady and now.

It seemed surreal!

Mary said let me have your phone number, I will have my sister call you ... Two weeks later no phone call with Mary stopping by the apartment to see what else I had accomplished in my decorating ... Asking me if I heard from her sister, I answered no she did not call. With that she states that I will make sure that she does call.

Two days later I received a call from Martha agreeing for me to pick her up in her apartment in Kew Gardens, Queens to meet for lunch at one of our local diners.

I pulled up to her apartment in my sports car Meeting her, she was prettier than I remembered.

Had a great lunch talking for hours then asking her out for diner for that Saturday night, with her accepting.

Could not believe that I was with this lady of my dreams!

We fell in love getting married ten months later on ...

A Christmas Day

TRIP TO PUERTO RICO

It is the middle of August in 2010 on a very hot day in Palm Desert, CA. My wife Martha and I were sitting in the family room watching TV when we received a phone call. Usually when I am home I answer the phone but with Martha being right next to the phone she answers the call. I hear her say yes this is she repeating that a few times, after a couple of minutes talking the conversation is over. Martha then relates the phone call saying that a gentleman named Eduardo who claims to be Gilberto Santa Rosa's agent was tracking down past members that were with Tito Rodriguez band, inviting them to Puerto Rico for a show. (As it was, Martha had been with the band for seven years).

Martha stated that Eduardo would be calling back, saying it all seemed fake. Two days later she receives another call from Eduardo asking her has she made up her mind regarding Puerto Rico … Martha's answer was no … Eduardo being very pervasive said he will call back in case she changes her mind.

Martha and I are discussing the calls saying maybe it's true … with that I looked up Gilberto Santa Rosa (as we both had never heard of him) to my surprise it turns out he is a mega star singer with Grammy awards in the Latin music field.

So we decided to take this one step further by calling Cindy Rodriguez in New Jersey who was Tito's Rodriguez daughter. Cindy proceeded to tell us that it is true that Gilberto is putting on a show in San Juan, wanting to bring back all of dad's old members of the band. Getting to play dad's music as Tito Nieves will be playing some of Tito Puente's songs. The concert is being called "The Palladium Home of the Mambo" it is going to be fantastic, you have to come to be part of the band … besides Gilberto is a sweetheart and he is going to pay for your entire trip to San Juan including a suite at the Condado Hotel. Everything is going to be 1st class, again insisting that she has to attend.

Martha tells Cindy that she will let her know … Martha and I discus going, finally agreeing that it will be a once in a life time opportunity to be reunited with the whoever was left from the band … All set. The next day Martha calls Eduardo stating that we will be going, he states that he will take care of making all the reservations including 1st class air with a suite at the hotel.

Now Martha is frantic she has to get fitted for two new costumes, remembering a local seamstress who she contacts agreeing to meet her for fittings. Ten days later the two costumes are ready for Martha to finalize … Martha came home all smiles with the costumes in hand.

We start talking about the trip and Martha says do not be surprised if I am going to be treated like a star when we get to Puerto Rico. (Yeah right I thought)!

Before you know it is September 10th the day we have to leave from Palm Springs airport boarding our plane, getting seated in 1st class. After two stops in Dallas then Miami it was on to San Juan, Puerto Rico arriving at 9:30 in the evening.

To our surprise Cindy Rodriguez is at the gate saying that Gilberto is double parked waiting for us. We continued to Gilberto's car with him getting out coming over to us. Cindy introduces Martha to Gilberto then to me … thinking he was going to shake my hand he proceeds to give me a big hug, stating it was a pleasure to meet me … WOW this coming from a super star.

We all got into his luxury Mercedes heading to the Condodo Hotel, checking into a beautiful suite. Compliments of Gilberto.

The next day Gilberto rents out a conference room at the hotel gathering all members of the band together for a quick reunion After about twenty minutes the main door opens and the press enters, interviewing Gilberto some of the band, then Martha. The next day in the local newspaper there is an article about Martha with her picture ... (Maybe Martha was right on her being a star)

The next day Martha was scheduled to attend a radio program where she participated as a guest, taking phone calls answering questions for the first hour ... then Gilberto joined the talk show for the second hour.

Gilberto and Marta at Radio Station

We then went to lunch at a local restaurant Gilberto and Martha were being asked for their autographs throughout the entire lunch. (Maybe Martha was right she was being treated like a star).

The afternoon was spent rehearsing for the show which was taking place tomorrow night Saturday at a big dance hall. The tickets had been selling for the last three weeks being sold out as the maximum capacity reached was 800.

Showtime ...

The venue was broken up into two segments, starting the show was Tito Nieves playing the music of Tito Puente ... He was wonderful.

Then it was time for Gilberto ... The band started playing Mama Guela with this que Gilberto came on from stage right at the same time Martha was coming in from stage left both singing and dancing to the great song that Tito Rodriguez used to open his concerts with. Meeting in the middle of the stage then turning facing the audience, the crowd erupting with cheers as everyone tried to gather close to the stage.

Mama Guela

The ballroom was rocking with excitement, Gilberto then started to sing Tito's favorite songs, with Martha fronting the band playing her maracas and doing her routine. The first segment ended with Cindy Rodriguez singing a duet with Gilberto. During the intermission the Mambo Aces performed their dancing routine, they were spectacular.

Marta and Cindy Rodriguez with Mambo Aces

The second set opened almost repeating the first, the night ended in a jubilant celebration with both Tito Nieves and Gilberto singing a duet together.

It turned out to be a spectacular night only having to repeat it tomorrow in Mayaquez, which was on the western tip of the island. Taking us about two and a half hours to drive.

The performance was to start at 4:00pm with us arriving in Mayaquez about 1:00 pm having enough time to make sure everything was set up and getting to relax.

The show started the same way with about 300 people attending, ending with everyone cheering not wanting them to finish.

Back to San Juan, unknown to me Gilberto called ahead to one of his favorite restaurants asking them to stay open for our late arrival which will be around 10:00pm. Arriving about that time we were greeted by the owners who lead us to a private table in the rear of the establishment. The proprietors could not do enough for us overwhelming us with service … …

It was great eating out with a star!

Finishing our wonderful dinner going back to our hotel suite only for Martha to collapse on the bed exhausted. It took the two remaining days left in San Juan for Martha to get back too feeling herself.

Our new friends Gilberto and his future wife Alexandria took us to the airport saying goodbye, at the same time Tito Nieves was getting ready to fly back to NYC. We all shared our goodbyes hoping to see each other again.

Tito Nieves, Alexandria, Gilberto, Martha and Ronnie

We boarded the plane thinking back what a great …

ROAD TO A CAREER

I t was a chilly night as I prepared to attend our Orange County basketball referee's meeting. The association is comprised of about 150 referees who were responsible to cover over 50 high schools within Orange County. The association officiated girls and boys basketball games from freshman to varsity. A handful of officials were associated with a major league baseball teams, comprising of front office personal, a coach and scouts from various major league teams.

The scout for the LA Dodgers in Orange County lived in San Clemente which is in South Orange County. The area is comprised of high schools, Jr and four year colleges. It was quite an undertaking. Dick needed help in order to cover this territory. He found out that I had played baseball asking me if I would help him, Dick said that he would teach me the Dodger way of grading there prospects. But first he had to get the OK from the front office. Naturally, I told him I would love to help him ... Before you know it Feb. 1st was upon us, that's when Jr. and four year colleges are allowed to start playing baseball (So the learning curve began).

We attended some Jr. College games together, Dick would go over the grading of position player's and pitchers. Judging there performance was a challenge in the beginning but then I became more confident attending games by myself. After each game I would call Dick; report what I had seen, especially if there were any promising prospects (if there was he would follow up).

I was with Dick for over two years until one summer day he asked me to cover a summer baseball tournament by myself. It was a pretty big tournament with allot of prestige's teams going to play ... I stated that it will be allot of work and I think he should take charge. Dick said that he was going to Las Vegas to play in an amateur/professional golf tournament. I told Dick that that was a bad decision he was on thin ice with the GM already for different infractions. Dick stated that as long as I can cover the tournament we would be OK. So off he went to Las Vegas and the golf tournament.

The baseball and Dick's Golf tournaments was over the same day, the next day we were together to go over my reports when Dick gets a phone call from Ben the scouting director for the Dodgers saying you have to get into the office ASAP.

Dick proceeded to go up to Dodger stadium for his meeting with Ben and Al the GM the meeting went from bad to unmanageable. It happened that Dick and the professional golfer he was playing with had won the tournament there picture was in the paper ... needless to say Al told his scouting director to find a new replacement for Dick as there went my stint with the Dodgers.

In the meantime; one of the basketball officials (Bill) was a scout for the Chicago White Sox, he managed the Anaheim American Legion baseball team. He asked me if I could help him be his coach, I said that would be great. So after Dick had been let go my stint with the Dodgers had ended so did our legion season.

Bill said that he wanted to introduce me to the West Coast Supervisor for the Kansas City Royals. I met with Rosie (real name Ross) we hit it off right away; after getting to know my background Rosie offered me an Associate scout's position with the team which started my 18 year career with the Kansas City Royals.

Well my tenure with the L.A Dodgers came to an end but I am with a new team. (It feels like I just got traded). Rosie went over the Royals grading system. We were looking for prospects, position players assigning a grading number, that player is graded on the 5 tools he has. For the pitchers, it was about 6 grades we had to assign them from velocity to poise.

The years went by as Rosie treated all the associated scouts' great. But I was not content because I wanted to be under a salary contract. I had to be patient and wait. It was a new era in the major leagues starting with the draft in 1965 and the signing of free agents. The high finance teams were against it (the NY Yankees and the St. Louis Cardinals etc.) the scouting had to be improved to allow us to know the players sign ability, what round you are projecting which would equate to a dollar figure.

The talent pool in Orange County was outstanding because great players surfaced such as the likes of Blyleven, Messersmidt, Aase, Carter, Templeton etc.; many more as I cannot name them all.

It all came to an end in 1974 when the major league scouting bureau came into existence.17 of the 24 major league teams had joined the association. Leading to terminating some of the full time and part time scouts including the commission scouts. Then it included 22 of the 24 teams so I was let go in 1978. My dreams were shattered but I guess that was progress a chance for the teams to save money, nothing I could do!

I moved to Palm Springs, CA staying in touch with Rosie, he also moved to the desert remaining friends as he was still with Kansas City.

It is 1983 the California Angels were making Palm Springs there spring trading headquarters after moving from Holtsville, CA.

The Angels had some Latin players on the team. My wife at one time was an entertainer with a very popular Latin band, she befriended one of the Latin players, the next thing you know we have a small group coming over for dinner and talking baseball.

Rob at the time was on the JV baseball team at the high school. They practiced near the Angels workout fields. When the Angels left their practice fields, they passed the high school fields as they would give my son a hard time. Robs teammates would say do you know who that was, Rob would say sure I do they had dinner with us last week. So Burt, Juan. Dickey, Louis and Angel were all the culprits harassing my son in jest. It was a great spring training.

The season was over for the JV team my son (who was not a prospect) was voted MVP player who was hitting close to 400 with a 6-1 pitching record. He was called up to the varsity team for the last few games of the season. The last game ended, Rob and I were walking off the field heading to my car. Rob stated that he needed a new first baseman's glove for next year.

Jeff the varsity coach who was walking behind us heard our conversation proceeding to say make sure it's an outfielder's glove since you are going to be my left fielder next year. We continued to walk to the car in silence, when we were inside the car my son blurted out I am not going to play next year. (Again my son is no prospect) … But grading Rob out as 1st basemen, he was a 5 fielder projected to a 6 and had a 4+ arm which was playable, but all the other grades were below average for a pro prospect. I decided to take a trip to Orange County as they still had one week left in there baseball season.

Tuesday I went to two games out of the four teams, no one was losing their first basemen. This left Friday as my last day before CIF playoffs begin.

So off I went to Mission Viejo HS, I was sitting in the 2nd row thinking of how I was going to approach the coach's when I heard someone shouting "Ronnie," "Ronnie" from the grand stands above me. I looked up it was Floyd my old boss from KC. He waived me up as I climbed the stairs sitting down beside him. He wanted to know what I was doing in this part of the area. I told him the story about Rob. Floyd then said that Mission was losing their first baseman, mentioning that KC was rehiring and if I was going to come into the area he would be interested in having me back. I said yes if it is under contract. Floyd stated that after the game we should go to his home in Fullerton, we will call Art the scouting director for KC. Sounded great!

The game was over we made our way down to the field, Floyd

introduced me to the manager and coach as his new area scout (WOW I did not even have a contract yet). We then started talking about Rob, the coach said that legion tryouts are here next Saturday morning at 10:00 am. I replied we will be here.

We arrived at Floyds home in Fullerton he proceeded to call Art speaking to him then giving me the phone to do the same, Art offered me a one year contract with a base salary and expense account, he was going to send me 5 copies of the contract in which I had to sign returning for his and the GM approval. So 1984 started my career again.

I received the contracts from KC the next week, reading them over signing all the copies and sending them back to KC.

It finally happened!

Saturday came we had to leave Palm Springs early to arrive in Mission Viejo by 10:00 am if not earlier. We got to the parking lot above the field at 9:45. Rob grabbed his tote bag with his baseball gear as we walked down a steep path to the playing field.

The manager and coach were telling the players where to go and what to do … telling Rob to go out to right field so he could shag batting practice. The players were hitting off of a machine that was ejecting batting practice fastballs.

It came time for them to call Rob, he was waiting in the hole for his time to hit. (Rob loved hitting off the machine) Finally it is Robs turn to get into the cage, he gets up lefty it takes Rob the first few pitches to get his timing down; then he starts hitting line drives all over the place. Continuing that for about ten more swings. I looked over at the coaches you can see their eyes light up with big smiles. The coaches tell Rob OK grab your 1st baseman's glove and get out to the field, but Rob replied but coach I did not get up righty yet … "That's OK" they replied.

He made the legion team as well as the starting 1st baseman for the varsity team not missing one game at first base in his two years at the school.

In his junior year the team went to the Sothern California CIF championship behind a wonderful pitching staff (in fact over the two year period every starting pitcher went to a division 1 college) quite an accomplishment!

On road to the CIF finals you have to win the first three games in your bracket in order to play for the championship. The semi-final game was against a top ranked opponent ranked number 2 in the section ...

The coaching staff opted to pitch Bobby, who was undefeated that year in order to advance. It turns out Bobby shut the team down and Mission Viejo was on their way to the CIF championship. The only problem now was they had to face the second ranked team in all of California Diamond Bar HS. The game ended on the short side of a 3-2 score ... as the saying goes, "wait till next year."

The following season the baseball team lost only three players from the 1985 team so the nucleus of the team was intact. The season came down to the last game of the season, they had to win for a shot at the playoffs---- in which they did. The play offs began with Mission winning their first game, now they are getting ready to play in the quarter finals, looming in there way was the number one team in the entire state of California, Diamond Bar HS which happened to be the team they lost to in the CIF championship last year.

It was played at Mission Viejo home field with the stands overflowing with spectators. The final score was 3-2 in favor of the home team ... it was the same score that they had lost to them last year. The game ended in a jubilant celebration looking and feeling like they had won the championship redemption was sweet as they piled on one another after the last out.

On to the semi-finals to play in Norwalk ... The starting pitcher was slated to be the big lefty ... but at the last minute they decided to pitch Eddie who said he is not mentally pre-paired to pitch but they stayed with their selection. Eddie could not get out of the first inning, in came Kyle the lefty, Mission was down by 5 runs. Kyle shut them down the rest of the game giving up only 2 hits; but they could not make up the five run deficit losing 5-3. Season over!

Back to scouting the summer league when Floyd and I came across a 6-1" right hand pitcher that was throwing an average major fastball. Andre finished his high school season making him eligible to be drafted. We really liked his makeup we offered him a contract, we had a problem he was only 17 we needed his parent's permission to sign with the team … Another stumbling block his parents did not speak any English … what to do? I told Floyd we can have my wife be the entrepreneur as she spoke three languages and Spanish was her native … he said great idea. So in essence my wife signed Andre, off he went to rookie ball at the end of his third year Andre was invited to our instructional league which is for our promising up and coming players.

While pitching at the camp he was showing an above major league fast ball with the Florida Marlins coming in to the league he was picked by them in the expansion draft. His stay with the Marlins was short lived since he was part of three player deal to San Diego which included Trevor, Andre and a third player to be named later for Gary Sheffield, great trade for everyone.

I guess some time or another a good prospect slips away like this one. The big left hand pitcher from Mission Viejo HS; he attended one of our open tryout camps. Kyle pitched in the Bullpen another scout and I were in charge of evaluating the pitchers, Kyle was throwing way below his average fastball and did not have a good session. We had to release him but before he left I asked him if he was feeling all right his reply was that he got up at 6:00 to attend water polo practice as he was literally drained.

He then enrolled in a Division III school in San Diego becoming there number one starter … Kyle still wanted to attend a Division I school, he had the blessings of his coach to release him if that was in his future.

The summer was winding down as were all the tournaments. There were two left in my area that I had to cover. I went to the first one stayed for infield and outfield catching a few innings, then I hustled over to Riverside City College to the Championship game of the Stan Musial tournament. To my surprise Kyle is pitching, he has a no hitter going into the 7th inning.

I did something that I have never done in all my years of scouting, after the seventh inning with Kyle walking back to dugout I got up and shouted "Atta a way to go Kyle" this after getting a nod from the lefty. A local Division I coach came over to me and asked who the lefty is, I proceeded to tell him that he is now pitching for a Division III school in San Diego ... The coach then asked if I would introduce him to Kyle after the game. The game ended with Kyle pitching a 9 inning no hitter. Kyle started walking off the field as I gained his attention asking him to meet me; which he did with the coach coming over introducing the both of them. They excused themselves.

Kyle went on to pitch for the Division I team the next year; as a junior he pitched them into the college world series in Omaha. Before the opening game in which he was slated to start Kyle gets a call from the California Angels; he is there first pick in the 1st round ... needless to say he does not get out of the first inning they lose that game and the next, so after two games they are flying home. Kyle started his pro career with the Angels but was latter traded to the Philadelphia Phillies.

It was great seeing Kyle achieve his goal of making and pitching in the majors but a little bitter sweet for me for not being able to sign Kyle for KC.

But there was one player that did not get away, but for a while I thought he did. I sent my second report in on the big 6' 1" first baseman from Irvine H.S. Bobby had an awesome senior year. He was approached by Notre Dame for football and a local Division I college team for baseball. He still went undrafted (as his sign ability was poor as he wanted to attend school). So Bobby opted for playing baseball going to the local division I team figuring to play in his freshman season. That was not going to happen as the schools first baseman eventually became the starting first baseman for LA

Dodgers for the next 13 years. So now Bobby wanted to get released so he can go on to play at another Division I school …

But the coach cut him and would not release him therefore Bobby had no other alternative but to attend a Jr. College as a sophomore, making him eligible for the next baseball draft. He had quite a sophomore season hitting 21 homers and playing a good solid 1st base as he became our number one pick in the 2nd round.

Bobby finally made his way to the majors. In his first full season he hit .284 with 24 HR's 20 doubles and 64 RBI. Proceeding to win the Rookie of Year in the American league in 1994 by gathering 25 of the 28 first place votes.

That winter I received a plaque and a letter from Topps congratulating me for signing Bobby, in being awarded the Rookie of Year in the American League … …

I was let go from the team because of the baseball strike of 1994 … Achieving that award was a wonderful way to end a career … It was a great experience never to be forgotten.

Ron Marino
KC Royals Baseball Scout

ROAD TO OFFICIATING FOOTBALL

I t was our second year living in Huntington Brach California I was at an impasse as what to do to stay in sports. My playing career was over in baseball as I wanted to stay active.

I thought how about refereeing basketball! I called the Orange County Officials Organization only being told that it was the start of football season and that Basketball will start in about three months but we have already started hiring new officials for football, if you can attend the mandatory on field scrimmage being held this Saturday at Savanah High School in Santa Ana, CA. you may register, the scrimmage starts at 9:00 am …

What could be so difficult I have been watching football for over a decade having season tickets for the New York Jets, I really knew my football (I thought)

Arriving at the high school early Saturday morning meeting the assistant commissioner of the association signing me up … receiving my football kit comprising of the rule and case book along with the study guide containing the 100 questions for the open book exam.

The class started with all the new officials gathering in one area, the instruction began teaching on field mechanics for two of the four official's positions, Umpire and Head Linesman. Our beginner group (which included first, second and third year officials) are on the field during the scrimmage held by the Soph Frosh team, (the scheduled called for a two man crew to work there games) we were going over what we should be doing during running plays, passing situations and kicks.

The veteran officials were working with the varsity unit.

During our first break I opened up the study guide looking at the first question saying to myself this is going to be a slam dunk (Surprise)! The first question has me stumped ... Well on to the second it was more difficult than the first ... Boy am I in trouble.

During our second break an official comes over to me and introduces himself stating that he is one of the instructors at the Monday night meetings. Jack then states he had seen me open the study guide as you had a questionable look on your face ... So here is the proposition ... ...

I will give you the answers to the test which has to be turned in this Monday, but you have to promise me that you will study, then on your own retake the test. Deal I replied ... ...

I' am attending the Monday night meeting learning that this is the second one of the seven. (The by-laws state that you can miss one meeting without an excuse) that means I have to make all the remaining five.

I turn in my open exam purposely missing a number of questions keeping my score at 84.

The assignments were given out as the first year officials had to work the chain crew ... I got assigned to work the chains at the Santa Ana Bowl, not realizing that only the top officials will do the games. I also get to attend the pre-game conference that the referee holds. Between my meetings and my assignments I learned a great deal gearing up for the close book test which comprised of 50 question's having to average 75 between the open book and the closed tests.

You had to pass in order to qualify for assignments the next season. I passed looking forward to my second year.

The second season is here, time to start attending the meetings. I received my schedule which included eight Soph Frosh games of the ten week season.

Having a great time learning more and more each week.. The

key is to study, study and to study more ... Especially the case book (as it illustrates the unusual plays that can occur).

This same season I signed up to do Pop Warner and Jr. All American football doing this for three years working there games with a three man crew with the most knowledgeable official as the referee (white hat). Learned allot especially from our mistakes ... During this period I had the most problems in my entire career of officiating which was covering thirty four years. As it came from the parents as the players were great.

The bi-laws of the Orange County Football Association states that that the first three years in the association you are on probation (meaning you can only work Soph Frosh games), starting the fourth through your sixth year you are approved and you can work both Soph Frosh and Junior Varsity. Starting your seventh year you are eligible to get certified to work varsity games.

I was studying the rule book every available minute I had, going to varsity games seeing how the crews worked together.

Determined to get certified before my seventh year, making up stamped evaluations cards to be given to the coaches so that they can evaluate me ... Really determined to officiate varsity. At this time I was a commission scout for the Kansas City Royals baseball team, Rosie was my immediate boss (being the west coast supervisor) who was also an official in long standings. Rosie was personal friends with the commissioner of the Association John McDonough (AFL Referee) setting up a luncheon were we tried to get me elevated to certified status. Not going to happen have to finish my sixth year which I did.

Starting my seventh year finally getting my schedule which included five varsity games as a Head Linesman. At the time all the varsity games were made up of a four man crew. I was at that position for the next two seasons getting a full schedule which comprised of ten varsity games plus some lower division ones. During my tenth year I was switched to Field Judge again with a full schedule, in addition being assigned three games as a referee (white hat).

In the interim the California Pro Football League was holding tryouts for back judges for their five man crew. I tried out (at the time I was pretty fast) making one of the two openings that were available and being assigned to a crew. The referee on the crew I was assigned to was also the athletic director and head baseball coach of a local high school being one that I covered for the Kansas City Royals ... So we had a good relationship right from the get go. I had a really good year as back judge, the season ended just before the high school one began.

The new high school season started so did the classes, to my surprise I was entered in the class with the referee's ... receiving my schedule getting four games as a referee (white hat) the rest at the field judge position.

The CIF playoffs consisting of three rounds before the championship game, up until this year they were officiated with a four-man crew but now they opted for a fifth man as a Back Judge just for the championship game. The commission of the Southern Section of the CIF office was also an official out of the Los Angeles Association who happened to be the Field Judge on our crew in the Pro California League. I worked the championship games at back judge (no one in our association had knowledge of that position except for the officials that were working the Pro League, with this knowledge I did the next four years). Two of them were at Angel Stadium. One of the games Compton vs Millikan High Schools went into overtime ... Great officiated game!

Starting the 12th year in the association I was given the opportunity in having my own crew which now consisted of five men (including the Back Judge) picking who was available from the certified officials making it the 25th crew staying intact as long as I stayed in the Association (What a great honor).

At the same time I was made one of the instructors teaching the sixth year officials as the association grew to 250 members.

Can it get any better ... I guess it had ... I was picked to be the back judge in the California Pro Championship game being played in San Jose, CA as part of a the six man crew … The entire unit was flown up to San Jose on a Saturday for the Sunday afternoon game.

Overall in my 34 years of officiating football I worked in 9 CIF Championship games and a host of playoff ones.

Ron Marino

Former Referee

Varsity Game as White Hat

ON TO BASKETBALL

B asketball started the second week of December just when my first football classes were over.

The by-laws were the same for basketball as they were for football. The first through the third years you are probation only working Soph Frosh games. This time the games were separated meaning you have to work a doubleheader, the freshman was the first game followed by the sophomore game.

The games were shortened by two minutes for each of the four quarters.

Being on probation for the three years, getting approved going into my fourth year now being able to work Junior varsity games. I was still approved going into my sixth season still not ever working a varsity high school contest when I get assigned to work a Division III college one. WOW I worked a college game before doing a high school one!

I reached my seventh year finally getting some varsity games also working the Junior college women's schedule.

I was in my tenth year and I was working a X-Mas tournament game In Villa Park, CA between them and Servite High Scholl. The game ends and Daryl comes into the locker room (usually no one enters) introducing himself as the NBA official (he being under Mindy Rudolph commissioner of officials for the NBA) Daryl is in charge of the summer program at Cal State for new officials trying out for the NBA. He was attending the game as his freshman son Ronnie was playing for Servite.

He stated that we both had great flair on the court and if Bob and I would like to try out for the NBA officiating on a part time basis that this coming summer it will be held at Cal State Dominguez. My reply was that I have a wonderful job that I cannot leave being area manager for a major manufacturer so I declined his offer but Bob my fellow official says yes with this Daryl gives him his business card telling him to call prior to the summer camp. Bob attended the summer camp and went on to get hired as a part time official later becoming full time.

Four years later Jim and I are working the Angelus League championship game between St. Francis at Servite High School in Anaheim, CA.

The game is over who walks into the locker room but Daryl (who is now the commissioner of the NBA), stating you guys worked a great game going on to say that the NBA is looking to go too three officials in all their games next year. (The PAC-10 is already having three men work there league games).

Daryl said I already spoke to you years ago, then Daryl turns to Jim and offers him his card, Jim accepts his invitation to workout at Cal State Dominguez.

The summer comes and Jim goes to the camp at Cal State trying out but to no avail as the NBA puts on hold going to a three man officiating crew They do implement this three years later … But Jim has moved out of the state.

Then I moved to the Coachella Valley living in Palm Springs, Ca. working basketball for the Southern Section Lower Desert Association. Leaving an area where we had over fifty high school hardly ever working the same school twice in one season. Going to a section where they had only eight high schools to cover so naturally we worked the same schools multiple times in one year. The association parred me up with Jeff who was a teacher and the head baseball coach at Palm Springs high school, the only games we could not work together were the ones for Palm Springs.

It was towards the end of my third year doing football officiating at the Desert Association and the playoffs were starting when I get a call from the assigner stating that he wants me along with Colin to work the Los Angeles Lakers scrimmage at College of the Desert. Off we go to work the closed scrimmage at C.O.D. WOW what a thrill getting to work a game with Kareem, Worthy, Scott, Cooper and Magic who was indeed magic making plays that I thought were impossible.

I refereed Jr. College and High School basketball for eighteen years always saying when I start to get rabbit ears (Getting to me) it would be time to hang it up …

I was officiating the Jr. College C.O.D. game against Mt. San Jacinto when I gave the coach from San Jacinto his second technical foul (which means he is ejected from the game) having to leave the playing area.

The game is over and I was walking off the court when the visiting coach comes storming out of the locker room approaching me yelling and screaming … with this we are eye ball to eye ball almost getting to the point of blows when assistant coaches from both teams pulled us apart … … As I promised myself eighteen years ago when it finally gets to me that's it … So that's it … That was my last game!

Looking back it was a great career officiating basketball no matter how it ended.

Ron Marino

Former Basketball Official

809 ARNOW AVE

It was a stickball game between two rival neighborhoods, being played in the street on Arnow Ave in the Bronx, which is our home field. If you can believe it we had spectators from our parents to neighbors. One of the spectators was a seven year old who was a skinny little girl with big brown eyes. Living at 809 Arnow Ave … Kind of cute if a seven year old is cute.

Our neighborhood was made up of different age groups. In our group we had about fourteen friends, but one was particularly close as we grew up practically brothers. Norman and I were best friends since we started going to elementary school together at PS #76 in the Bronx. Norm lived in the same building that little Debbie lived in at 809 Arnow Ave. Norms grandparents who owned the five family building lived on the second floor in one of the two apartments which Norman and his parents lived in the other one.

We continued to play almost all the sports together from our basketball team (which comprised of eight of our friends) playing in a league we also played two hand touch football on Arnow Ave. but our favorite was called over the line in other areas … but we called it mush ball! On rainy days we went to the pool room to play pool (we probably went on sunny days also)

Norman bottom right

The stickball field as mentioned was on Arnow Ave as home plate being the sewer cover which is almost perpendicular from the steps leading up to the five family home at 809 Arnow Ave.

Debbie was always either sitting on the stoop or standing cheering us on. After every game she would come over wanting to talk (especially to me).

This skinny little girl use to come over to my apartment asking my parents if she can walk our wire hair fox terrier. Of course my parents would comply. This went on for a few years Debbie was always the little girl in my eyes.

We graduated from high school, after graduation Norman's family moved to Queens New York, Norman enrolled in Queens Poly Technical College (to study engineering). The same time Norman's grandparents sold the five bedroom house at 809 Arnow Ave to Debbie's grandparents.

Debbie's parents moved to the second floor taking over Norman's old apartment and Debbie's grandparents taking the other apartment.

The years went by as I attended NYU after two semesters I joined the US Army … So here it is 1961 and I'm living in New Jersey wanting to move back to the old neighborhood in the Bronx.

I get to my old neighborhood and I see some of my old friends, we start talking ... ... I see this girl walking down the street turning the corner and disappearing. She was wearing a mini-skirt with a beautiful blouse her blonde hair flowing down over her shoulders. Wow what a pretty lady ... I proceeded to ask my friends who that was, they replied it is Debbie ... I say who is Debbie? They replied Debbie was the little girl who use to walk your dog. That was the skinny little girl with the big brown eyes ... WOW did she grow up!

I have to meet her (knowing that she lived in 809 Arnow Ave) ... How am I going to do that?

As it turns out my father was renting one of the three garage spaces that were attached to 809 Arnow, they were at the bottom of the alley. There is three identical buildings in a row 805, 807 and 809 Arnow Ave. all having similar three car garage spaces each having driveways leading down the alley.

I decided to park my little sports car blocking one of the driveways (which happened to be the one at 809 Arnow Ave) knowing that whoever can use the other two driveways were still able to get to their cars if needed.

I called my friend Richie who lived directly across from 809, asking him to let me know if and when Debbie was outside her house. Richie called me as his window faced the street as he can see across to at 809 Arnow Ave ... telling me that Debbie was sitting on the stoop in front of her house.

Time to try and meet Debbie ... Here goes ... I approached the driveway towards my sports car when Debbie says "you cannot park your car there" I retaliate but my father is renting one of the garage below ... "Well you cannot park there as my grandmother owns the building."

After the dust settles Debbie and I ride out to Orchid beach with the top down as it is a warm summer night. I placed a blanket on the sand, we talked and talked with the small waves in the background, making it very romantic. Before you know it we are in each other's arms ... what a glorious night!

Our relationship lasted for about two years ... We were talking about marriage when the aspect of children came up with Debbie being Jewish and I Catholic. We had to figure out how to raise the children ... We agreed that they should decide for themselves ... All set! I thought ...

Until one night I get a phone call from Debbie at 9:30 saying that she wants to talk to me ... I said go ahead, but she states I would like it to be in person ... So I walk over to 809 Arnow Ave. Debbie proceeded to tell me that she spoke to her grandmother and parents they all agreed that if we had children that they would have to be brought up Jewish ...

I am beside myself ... my comment was an affirmative NO. If you insist on this we cannot think of getting married. Debbie held her ground and so did I.

Six months later Debbie met Harvey her future Jewish husband, we were finished. I then met Martha my future wife getting married in 1966.

It was 1994 I was separated from my wife, when I reached out to my married friends Mike and his wife Judy, who knew some of Debbie's friends ... One in particular gave us Debbie's phone number ... calling Debbie finding out she lived in North Miami ... We communicated on the phone for about a month. Then there was a period of close to three weeks that I could not reach her. Finally reaching Debbie only to find out that her 27 year old daughter passed away ... I was really sadden by this news, stating that I will fly to Miami to be with her at this sorrowful time. I was met by Debbie, picking me up at the Miami airport. I stayed a little over a week getting to see her mother at her condo in Aventura FL and her dad who was in a home, with him only having a short time to live ... it was great seeing them both as it had been thirty years.

I flew back to California and about two months later I reconciled with my wife.

It is now the later part of 2015 my wife gets diagnosed with a rare form of leukemia being given about three or four months to live … She passed away in February of 2016.

It was 2017 I am living in Palm Desert CA when one day I received a call from a number I did not recognize … hello I said, the male response says are you Ron and I answered yes … did you live in the Bronx again my reply was yes … Did you live near Arnow Ave again repeating yes … finally saying who is this as he proceeds to say Norman and I yell out his last name.

Norman and another friend tracked me down as I have not heard from my dear old friend for over 65 years … 65 years and they found me … What a surprise … Great day!!!!

We make arraignments for me to fly to Florida where he has a winter home in Boynton Beach his main home in Annapolis Maryland

Because of some personal complications the trip was put on hold until 2019, sin March of that year it was off to Florida as both Norm and his wife Barbara met me at the West Palm Beach airport.

We arrived at their beautiful home in Boynton Beach ... bringing up things from the past. We began talking about the old neighborhood when Debbie's name came up ... Norman could not remember her ... though he asked me do you know where she lives, or do you have her last name ... I replied yes stating her last ... with that Norm started to search for her phone number on the internet coming up with a number having a New York prefix ...

The next day I called the number with a woman answering ... I did the same thing that Norman did to me, final saying this is Ronnie ... with that Debbie lets out a scream yelling my last name.

We make arraigments to meet in a couple of days, I taking the Amtrak from the Boynton Beach station to the Hollywood station in Florida ... Taking about fifty minutes ... Debbie met me at the rail station as we then went for a wonderful lunch by the beach ...

Returning back to Norm's house in Boynton Brach ...

We discussed my luncheon with Debbie proceeding to remind him that Debbie's grandparents bought the five family house from his grandparents and that Debbie moved in to his old apartment ... Probably sleeping in the same room ... Wow what a turn of events.

Before you know it, it was time to leave my special friends ... As we stayed in contact.

Another year passing with me taking another trip in February of 2020 flying into West Palm Beach, as one of Norm's friend's picked me up taking me to Norm's home ... I stayed with Norm for a week, then Debbie picked me up from Norms. After a late lunch we headed back to Debbie's condo in Aventura ... Her mother passed away and Debbie inherited the two bedroom condo which was on the 21st floor of a 22nd story building ... having a great view of the channel and the Atlantic Ocean.

It was a wonderful two weeks enjoying being with Norman and his wonderful wife Barbara, meeting Debbie, getting to know some of her friends … Well back to California …

Still staying in contact with my two old friends. Looking towards the day that the virus is under control so I can travel again, to plan another trip to Florida so we can remanence about … … 809 Arnow Ave

…

Debbie

Printed in the United States
by Baker & Taylor Publisher Services